HANUKKAH

The Jewish festival of Hanukkah, or Chanukah, is also called [ ] for eight days and usually occurs in December, although in [ ] November. It commemorates not only the triumph of the Maccabees over the great army of the Syrian king, Antiochus IV, in 165 B.C., but also the universal message that all people have the right to be free.

After the Jews had won their battle, they went to their temple and found that the Syrians had brought in statues of their own gods. The eternal light had been allowed to go out. The Jews rekindled the light, but they had only enough oil to keep it burning for one day, and it would take eight days for a messenger to get more oil. The miracle of Hanukkah is that the oil kept burning for eight days, long enough for the messenger to return with more. Jews use a candleholder called the menorah to symbolize this miracle. It holds nine candles. One, the shammash, is used to light the others. They stand for the eight days that the oil kept burning.

Hanukkah is celebrated by lighting the candles of the menorah, playing games of chance with a spinning top called a dreidel, and eating special holiday foods such as potato pancakes called latkes. Children often receive a gift on each night of Hanukkah in addition to Hanukkah gelt (money). This gelt sometimes consists of chocolate wrapped in gold foil to look like money.

Activities

✡ Give a Hanukkah party in your classroom. This can be very simple or very festive, but it should include at least one traditional food, some gelt, a chance to play the dreidel game, and the singing of some Hanukkah songs. You can give one yourself with the help of a Jewish delicatessen. Gelt can be purchased everywhere in its little net bags. Directions for playing the dreidel game can be found on page 4. Read Hannukah stories. Have children make Hanukkah hats to wear for the party. See pages 11-14. Buy inexpensive plastic dreidels for your students or have each student make his or her own. (See page 4.)

✡ Beautiful Hanukkah cards can be made easily. Fold blue paper into a card shape. Lay the cut-out shape of a candle on the front of the card. Lightly sponge thin white tempera paint over the entire front. Carefully lift away the candle. Allow to dry and write a message inside. (See page 5.)

✡ Let children make a menorah using frosting and marshmallows. Give each child a piece of tagboard 11" x 4" (28cm x 10cm), ten marshmallows, and nine candles. Have the children spread some white frosting on the bottom of each marshmallow and then put them onto the tagboard. With the frosting, "glue" a second marshmallow on top of the middle marshmallow to create the shammash or "servant." Poke birthday candles into each marshmallow to create a menorah.

Bibliography

My First Chanukah by Tomie DePaola. (Putnam, 1989)

A Picture Book of Hanukkah by David A. Adler (Holiday, 1982)

Latkes and Applesauce by Fran Manushkin (Scholastic, 1992)

HANUKKAH!

Author: Roni Schotter

Publisher: Joy Street/Little, Brown & Company, 1990 (Canada, UK: Little Brown; AUS, Penguin).

Summary: This delightfully illustrated book tells the story of a modern-day family's celebration of Hanukkah and the joy it brings to the family, especially the young children.

Related Holiday: Hanukkah, or the Festival of Lights, has been celebrated by Jewish people around the world for 2,000 years. It lasts for eight days and comes at the end of November or in December. Hanukkah is a holiday to celebrate the victory of Judah Maccabee over King Antiochus for the right to worship their own God. When the Jewish people won the battle, they celebrated for eight days. Although only enough oil to light the menorah for one day was found, the oil burned for eight days.

Related Poetry: "Hanukkah Candles" by Jean Warren, *Small World Celebrations* (Warren Publishing House, 1988).

Related Songs: "Hanukkah, Hanukkah" by Carla C. Skjong, "Eight Little Candles" by Jean Warren, and "I'm a Little Dreidel" (adapted traditional), *Holiday Piggyback Songs* (Warren Publishing House, 1988).

Connecting Activities:

✡ To build your students' knowledge about Hanukkah, plan to read (or have available for students' independent reading) several factual books about this holiday, such as *My First Chanukah* by Tomie Depaola, *A Picture Book of Hanukkah* by David A. Adler, *All About Hanukkah* by Judye Groner and Madeline Wikler, and *Latkes and Applesauce* by Fran Manushkin. (See bibliography, page 1.)

✡ Invite a guest speaker to come into your classroom to explain the history of Hanukkah and how Hanukkah is celebrated in his or her home. If some of your students celebrate the holiday they can share their experiences.

✡ List with your students the ways that the family in *Hanukkah!* celebrated the holiday. Be sure to include lighting the menorah, eating latkes, playing dreidel *(dray dl)* games, and giving gifts.

✡ During the story, the older boy teaches his younger brother to say "Hanukkah" correctly. Help students to learn the correct pronunciation *(hon oo kah).*

✡ Encourage your students to make their own special signs for Hanukkah similar to the one in the story that the young girl made. Save these to display on the "Happy Hanukkah" bulletin board described on the next page.

✡ The last two pages of *Hanukkah!* give a useful summary of the story of Hanukkah and words which are unique to this celebration. Explain the significance of the menorah and the shammash to Hanukkah. Bring in a real menorah and shammash to share with your students and to illustrate the lighting of the menorah.

✡ Make a large menorah (candle holder with nine branches) on a "Happy Hanukkah" bulletin board as the center of your Hanukkah celebration. Use bright blue paper for the background, and gold foil wrapping paper cut into the shape of the menorah. Use cardboard paper towel tubes covered with white or colorful paper for the candles. Attach a yellow construction paper flame at the top of each candle. Place the shammash (helper candle) a little higher than the other candles and in the center of the menorah. Add another candle to the menorah each day during the eight days of your celebration.

✡ Purchase plastic dreidels for each student or make dreidels using the directions on page 4. Explain the basic game to your students. Play dreidel games in small groups.

✡ Challenge your students to make a class chart to compare and contrast Hanukkah, Christmas, and Kwanzaa. Children should notice that all involve gift-giving and feasting and all three celebrations fall within the same months. As to the differences, children should consider the length, the dates, traditional foods, and the history of each celebration.

Hanukkah	Kwanzaa	Christmas
Eight days long. **Give gifts.**	**Eight days long.** **Give gifts.**	**One day long.** **Give gifts.**

✡ Make latkes, the traditional potato pancakes fried in oil, which are served during Hanukkah. The oil is used to remember the oil that burned for eight days instead of one. A recipe for latkes may be found on page 8 or in the book *Latkes and Applesauce* by Fran Manushkin (Scholastic, 1990).

✡ Applesauce is the traditional complement for latkes. Make some homemade applesauce to enjoy with your latkes during the final day of your Hanukkah celebration.

THE DREIDEL GAME

Directions: Cut out the dreidel. Make holes as shown below. Fold along the inside lines to make a box. Fold the tabs inward. Use glue or tape to hold the dreidel together. Push a pencil or pen through the holes. Spin the dreidel and begin play.

To Play the Game

The dreidel is a four-sided spinning top. The letters written on the side of the dreidel are Hebrew for "A Great Miracle Happened There." Each symbol represents a different instruction for the game. To play, give each person a designated number of markers (gelt, candy, nuts, etc.) Each player puts one marker in the center, or "kitty," each time the dreidel is spun. Players take turns spinning the dreidel.

If the dreidel lands on:

| The player receives half of the kitty. | The player receives the whole kitty. | The player does nothing. | The player must put one marker in the kitty. |

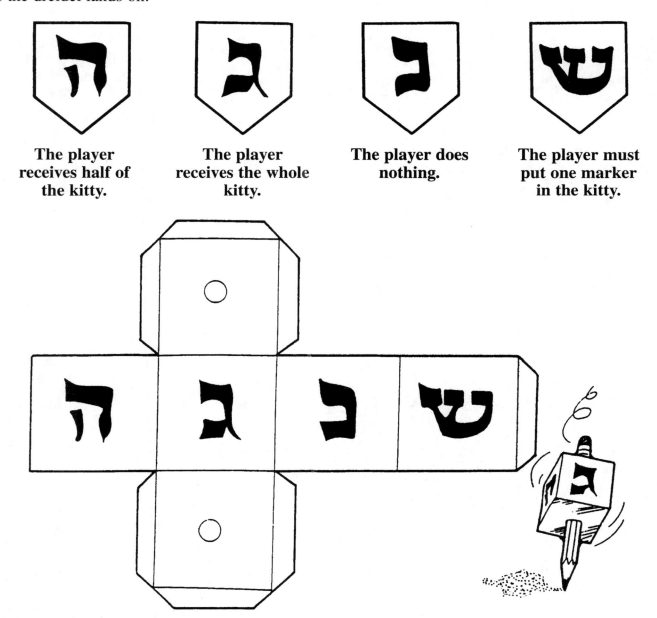

MAKING A HANUKKAH CARD

Materials:

- ✡ blue construction paper
- ✡ candle pattern
- ✡ white tempera paint
- ✡ paintbrush or sponge

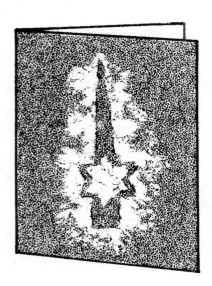

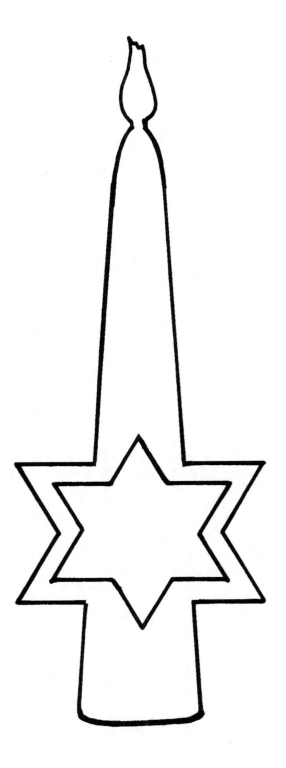

Directions:

Cut out the candle. Place it on the card. Sponge thin white tempera over and around the candle. Carefully remove the candle shape. Write a message inside the card.

HANUKKAH GARLAND

1. Reproduce, color, and cut out the pieces on this page. Cut the side slits on each piece.

2. Cut many ³⁄₄" x 5" (1.9cm x 12.70cm) strips of colored construction paper.

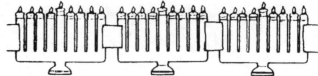

3. Connect the pieces together by making colored construction paper "rings." (See the diagram.)

4. Make a long chain to decorate your classroom!

MUSIC AND MOVEMENT

"One Little, Two Little, Three Little Candles"
(Sing this song to the tune of "One Little, Two Little, Three Little Indians.")
One little, two little, three little candles,
Four little, five little, six little candles,
Seven little, eight little, nine little candles,
In my Hanukkah lamp.
The first night, one little candle,
The second night, two little candles,
The third night, three little candles in my Hanukkah lamp.
The fourth night, four little candles,
The fifth night, five little candles,
The sixth night, six little candles in my Hanukkah lamp.
The seventh night, seven little candles,
The eighth night, eight little candles,
The shammash makes nine little candles in my Hanukkah lamp.

Sing "One Little, Two Little, Three Little Candles" again. This time line up eight children and have them all curl over or squat down. Choose another child to be the shammash. As the song is sung, the shammash lightly taps each "candle," who then rises.

Repeat, letting all children have a turn to be candle.

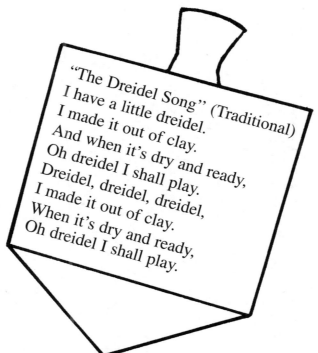

"The Dreidel Song" (Traditional)
I have a little dreidel.
I made it out of clay.
And when it's dry and ready,
Oh dreidel I shall play.
Dreidel, dreidel, dreidel,
I made it out of clay.
When it's dry and ready,
Oh dreidel I shall play.

Let children spin around as if they were dreidels. One child can start out in a crouching position, and another can pretend to be turning him or her. As the top spins faster, the child gets to spin more.

FOOD EXPERIENCES

Potato Latkes (Pancakes)

To remember the oil that lit the lamp, fried foods are served at Hanukkah time. Potato pancakes, called latkes, are one of the traditional foods. Try these with your class, using an electric skillet, but remember to use extreme caution around the hot oil.

- ✡ 2 cups (475 mL) peeled and grated potatoes
- ✡ 2 teaspoons (10 mL) grated onion
- ✡ 1 egg
- ✡ 6 Tablespoons (90 mL) flour
- ✡ 4 Tablespoons (60 mL) oil

Mix together all ingredients except oil. Heat oil in a pan. Drop a tablespoon (15 mL) of the mixture into oil. Cook and turn once until brown on both sides. Applesauce and sour cream go well with latkes.

Applesauce

Wash and peel five apples. Cut into quarters and remove the cores. Put the pieces into a saucepan and add ¾ cup (177mL) of water. Cover and simmer until tender. Let the apples cool. Let children take turns mashing the apples with a potato masher or mixer. Add sugar and cinnamon to taste.

Doughnuts

Doughnuts, another food prepared in oil, are served during Hanukkah in parts of the world. Serve this treat to your children. Doughnut holes work especially well for young children.

MENORAH PATTERN

Reproduce the menorah pattern once and the candles nine times. Have children color and cut out. Glue the menorah onto construction paper. Glue candles into each branch of the menorah. If you are doing this during the days of Hannukah let children glue one candle on each day.

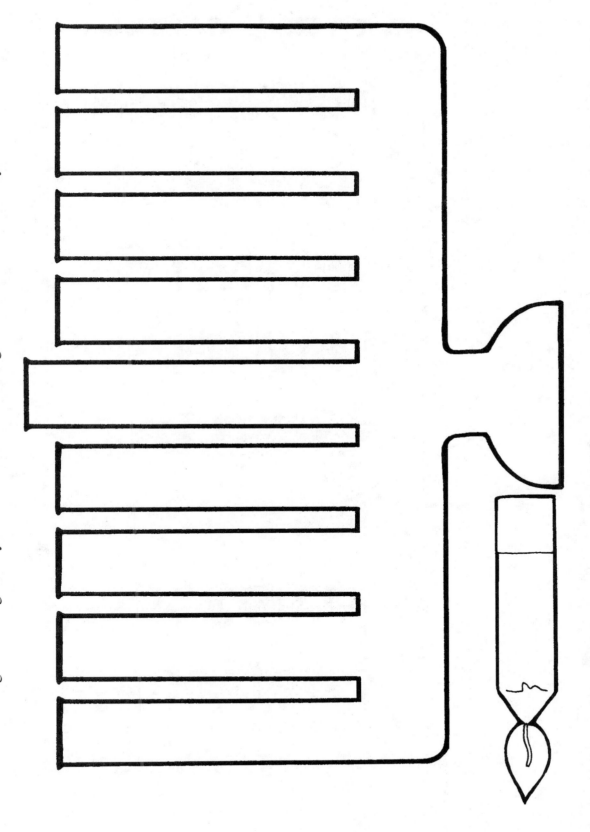

YOU CAN DRAW IT!

Copy the picture one square at a time onto the bottom grid. Color your picture when you have finished your drawing.

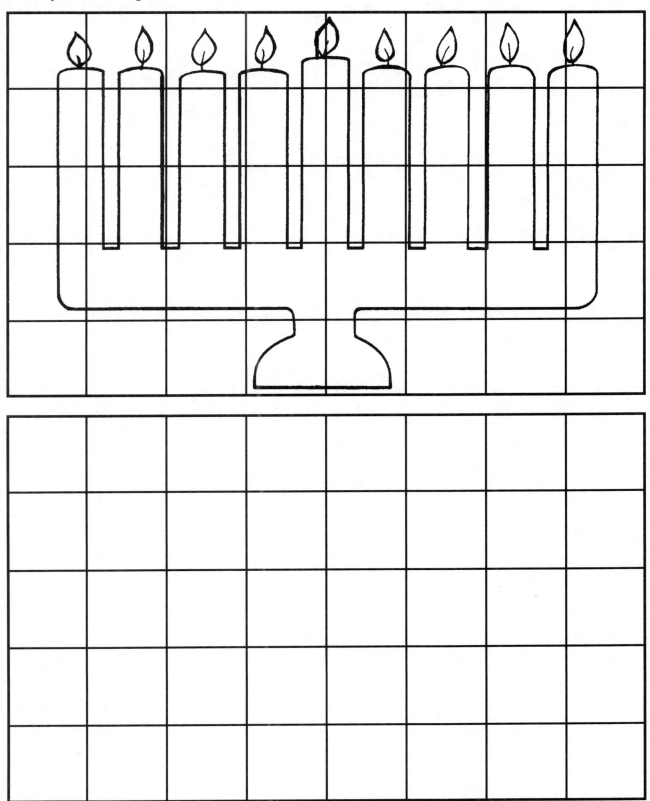

10

HANUKKAH HAT

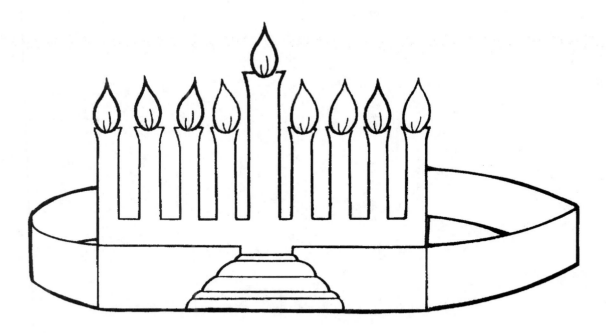

Directions:

1. Copy, color, and cut out all pattern pieces.

2. Glue each flame to a candle wick.

3. Glue the sides to the front where marked.

4. Fit the menorah to the child's head, stapling the headband at the back.

Creative Suggestions:

✡ Use foil paper for the candles.

✡ Use tissue for the flame, or glue crumpled tissue to the flame.

✡ Add glitter to the menorah.

✡ Add a desert scene to the side panels with the palm trees.

Menorah

Cut 1

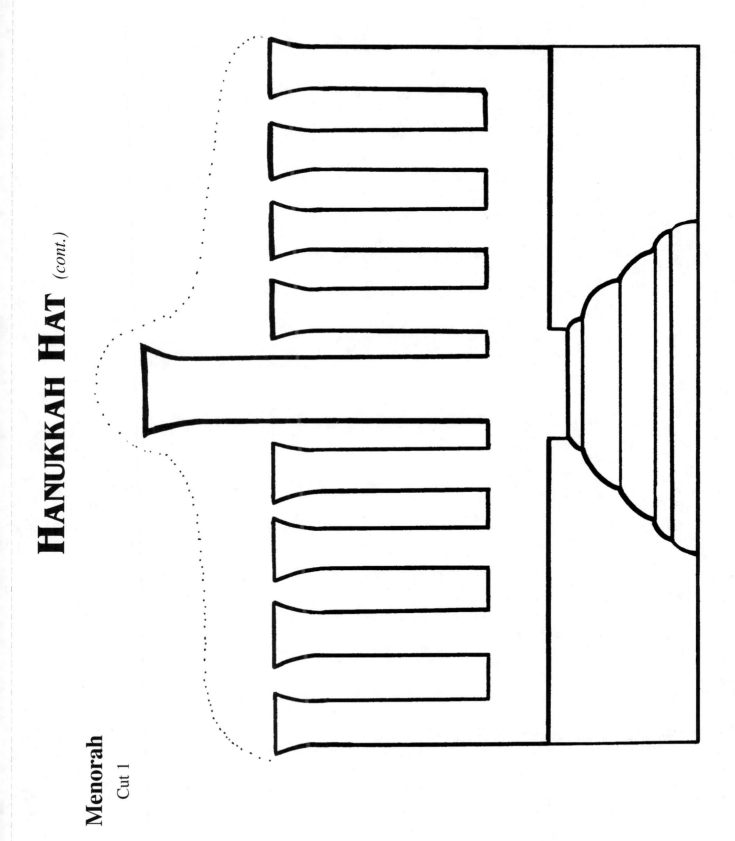

HANUKKAH HAT *(cont.)*

Headband -
Right Side
Cut 1

HANUKKAH HAT *(cont.)*

Flames
Cut 9 Total

**Headband -
Left Side**
Cut 1

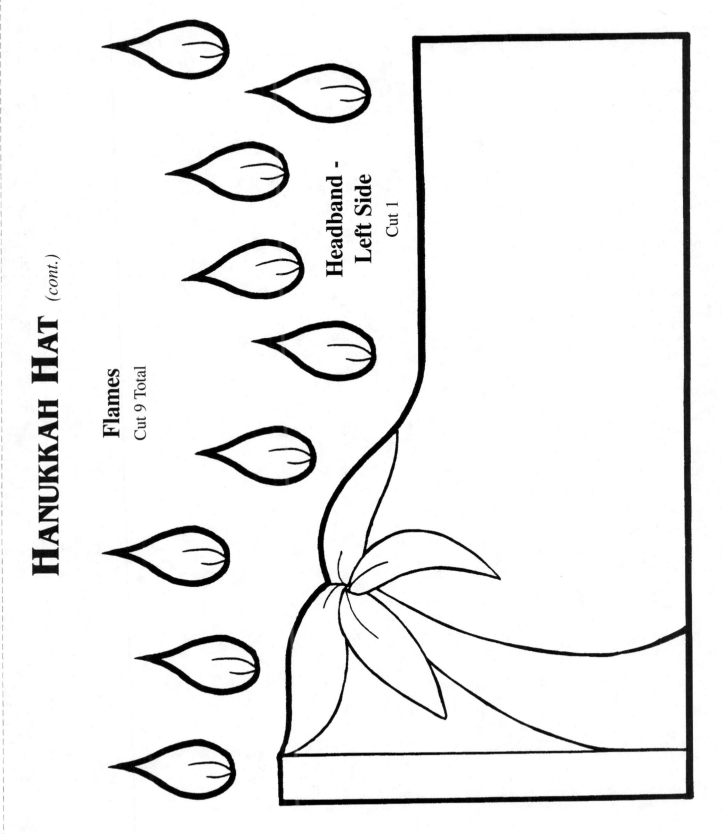

STAR OF DAVID

Materials Needed:

- ✡ glue
- ✡ scissors
- ✡ hole punch
- ✡ string
- ✡ glitter (optional)
- ✡ two contrasting colors of construction paper

Directions

1. Reproduce "star" pattern on two contrasting colors of construction paper. Reproduce two of each color for each child.

2. Cut out outer triangle.

3. Fold each triangle on dotted line.

4. Cut folded triangle on solid inner line then unfold. Repeat on remaining triangles.

5. Glue two contrasting triangles together, one pointing up and one pointing down. Repeat with second set of contrasting triangles.

6. Put glue along dotted lines remaining on stars. Glue two stars together along dotted lines only. Allow to dry.

7. When dry, fold left and right points toward the middle, front and back.

8. Punch hole in top and hang with string.

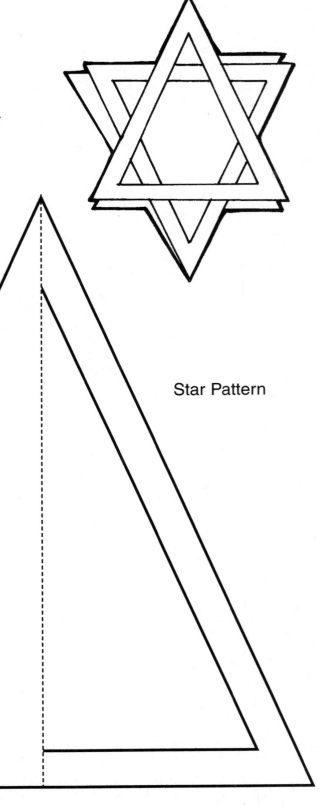

Star Pattern

HANGING DREIDEL

Reproduce both pieces of the dreidel onto index paper. Decorate. Slit the pieces on the dashed lines and slip the pieces together as shown. Tape them in the creases. Punch a hole in the top. Thread a piece of yarn or string and hang as a decoration.

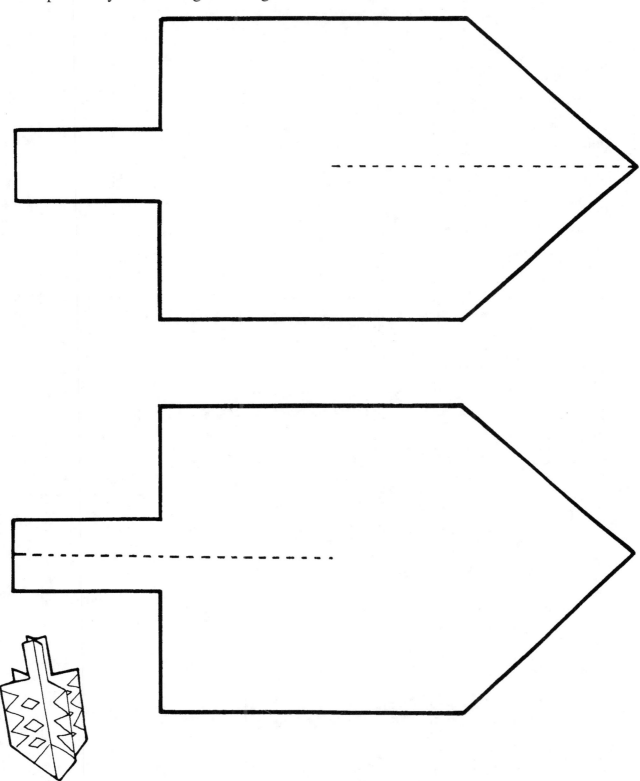